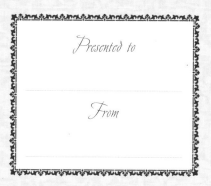

Presented to

From

A GIFT OF

Comfort

for a Hurting Heart

Stories for the Heart *Mini* Books

COMPILED *by* ALICE GRAY

Multnomah Gifts™
Multnomah® Publishers Sisters, Oregon

A Gift of Comfort for a Hurting Heart
a Stories for the Heart *Mini* Book

© 2002 by Multnomah Publishers, Inc.
published by Multnomah Gifts™, a division of Multnomah® Publishers, Inc.
P.O. Box 1720, Sisters, Oregon 97759

ISBN 1-59052-028-9

Designed by Koechel Peterson & Associates, Minneapolis, Minnesota

Multnomah Publishers, Inc., has made every effort
to trace the ownership of all poems and quotes.

In the event of a question arising from the use of a poem or quote,
we regret any error made and will be pleased to make
the necessary correction in future editions of this book.

Please see the acknowledgments at the back of the book
for complete attributions for this material.

Scripture quotations are taken from *The Holy Bible*,
New International Version © 1973, 1984 by International Bible Society,
used by permission of Zondervan Publishing House.

Multnomah is a trademark of Multnomah Publishers, Inc.,
and is registered in the U.S. Patent and Trademark Office.
The colophon is a trademark of Multnomah Publishers, Inc.

All rights reserved. No portion of this book may be reproduced
in any form without the written permission of the publisher.

Printed in China

02 03 04 05 06 07 08—10 9 8 7 6 5 4 3 2 1 0

www.multnomahgifts.com

TABLE OF CONTENTS

Comforting

Charles Swindoll

A little girl lost a playmate in death and one day reported to her family that she had gone to comfort the sorrowing mother.

"What did you say?" asked her father.

"Nothing," she replied, "I just climbed up on her lap and cried with her."

The soul would have no rainbow
had the eyes no tears.

AUTHOR UNKNOWN

Words Must Wait

Don't talk to me yet;

the wound is fresh,

the nauseous pain

I can't forget

fades into numbness

like a wave,

then comes again.

Your tears I understand,

but grief is deaf;

It cannot hear the words

you gently planned

and tried to say.

But…

pray.…

RUTH BELL GRAHAM

A Single Crocus

Joan Wester Anderson

*I*t was an autumn morning shortly after my husband and I moved into our first house. Our children were upstairs unpacking, and I was looking out the window at my father, who was moving around mysteriously on the front lawn. My parents lived nearby, and Dad had visited us several times already. "What are you doing out there?" I called to him.

He looked up, smiling. "I'm making you a surprise." Knowing my father as I did, the "surprise" could be just about anything. When we were kids, he once rigged up a jungle gym out of wheels and pulleys. A self-employed jobber, he was always building things out of odds and ends. For one of my Halloween parties, he created an electric pumpkin and mounted it on a broomstick. As guests came to our door, he would light the pumpkin and have it pop out in front of them from behind the bushes.

Today, however, Dad would say no more. As I became caught up in the busyness of our new life, I eventually forgot about his surprise.

That is, until one raw day the following March when I glanced out the window. Dismal. Overcast. Little piles of dirty snow still stubbornly littering the lawn. Would winter ever end?

And yet…was it a mirage? I strained to see

∽o∾

14

what looked like something pink, miraculously peeking out from beneath a drift. And was that a dot of blue across the yard, a small note of optimism in this gloomy expanse? I grabbed my coat and headed outside for a closer look.

They were crocuses, scattered whimsically throughout the expanse of front lawn. Lavender, blue, yellow, and my favorite, pink—little, bright faces bobbing in the bitter wind.

Dad. I smiled, realizing he had secretly planted the bulbs last fall. He knew how the darkness and dreariness of winter always got me down. What could have been more perfectly attuned to my needs? How blessed I was, not

only for the flowers, but for his love.

My father's crocuses bloomed each spring for the next four or five seasons, bringing that same assurance every time they arrived: *Hard times are almost over. Hold on, keep going, light is coming soon.*

Then came a spring with only half the usual blooms, and the next spring there were none. I missed the crocuses, but my life was busier than ever. Besides, I had never been much of a gardener. I thought I would ask Dad to come over and plant new bulbs. But I never did.

He died suddenly, one gray October day. My family grieved deeply, leaning on our faith.

I missed him terribly, though I knew he would always be a part of us.

Four years passed, and on a dismal spring afternoon I was running errands and found myself feeling depressed. *You've got the winter blahs again*, I told myself. *You get them every year; it's chemistry.* But it was something else, too.

It was Dad's birthday, and I found myself thinking about him. This was not unusual— my family often talked about him, how he had lived his faith. Once I saw him take off his coat and give it to a homeless man. Often he'd chat with strangers passing by his storefront, and if he learned they were poor and hungry, he would

invite them home for a meal. But now, in the car, I couldn't help wondering, *How is he now? Where is he? Is there really a heaven?*

I felt guilty for having doubts. *But sometimes,* I thought as I turned into our driveway, *faith is so hard.*

Suddenly I slowed, stopped, and stared at the lawn. Muddy grass and small gray mounds of melting snow. And there, bravely waving in the wind, was one pink crocus.

How could a flower have bloomed from a bulb more than eighteen years old, one that had not blossomed in over a decade? But there was the proof. Tears filled my eyes as I realized

the significance of that single crocus. *Hold on, keep going, light is coming soon.*

The pink crocus bloomed for only a day. But it built my faith for a lifetime.

❦

Winter is on my head, but eternal spring is in my heart.

AUTHOR UNKNOWN

∞∞∞

Down in my solitude under the snow,

Where nothing cheering can reach me,

Here, without light to see how to grow,

I'll trust nature to teach me.

From my heart will young buds diverge,

As rays of the sun form their focus;

And I from the darkness of earth shall emerge,

A happy and beautiful crocus!

Gaily arrayed in my pink and green,

When to their view I have risen,

Will they not wonder how one so serene

Came from so dismal a prison?

Many, perhaps, from so simple a flower

This useful lesson may borrow,

Patient today through its gloomiest hour,

We come out the brighter tomorrow.

HANNAH F. GOULD

At the Winter Feeder

His feather flame doused dull

by ice and cold,

the cardinal hunched

into the rough, green feeder

but ate no seed.

Through binoculars I saw

festered and useless

his beak, broken

at the root.

Then two: one blazing, one gray,

rode the swirling weather

into my vision

and lighted at his side…

Unhurried, as if possessing

the patience of God,

they cracked sunflowers

and fed him

beak to wounded beak

choice meats.

Each morning and afternoon

the winter long,

that odd triumvirate,

that trinity of need,

returned and ate

their sacrament

of broken seed.

JOHN LEAX

I have a God

who hears me,

I have a God

who's near.

I have a God

who's waiting

with a bottle for my tears.

KIMBER ANNIE ENGSTROM

∽∘∾

Because of the LORD's great love

we are not consumed,

for his *compassions* never fail.

They are *new every morning;*

great is your faithfulness.

LAMENTATIONS 3:22–23

Salvaged and Restored

Ruth Bell Graham

*H*e had built for himself a great house that was a thing to behold. It was a masterpiece of salvaged materials.

He collected and sold scrap metal as well as antiques, and he was fascinated with broken bits and pieces of china dug from his front yard. Carefully he fitted and glued the pieces together. Few objects ever came out whole. They were simply the collection of one who cared. I expressed an interest in his work and he gave me a blue-and-white plate that had been carefully glued together, despite pieces that were missing. I commented, "You remind me of God." I knew from the look on his face that I had shocked him and I hurried to explain: "God takes our broken lives and lovingly pieces them together again. Even if a piece has been lost, God gathers what He can and restores us to wholeness in Him."

❧

"For I know the plans I have for you," declares the LORD, "plans to prosper you and not to harm you, plans to give you hope and a future."

JEREMIAH 29:11

A Pair of Worn-Out Shoes

Thelda Bevens

his morning it was his shoes. I was rounding up the garbage and sorting the recycle items, carrying them down to the street and looking around the place for any I had missed. Since the garbage can was only half full (another reminder of how much has changed), I wandered into that place where junk abounds—the garage.

The first item I tossed away was the broken snow shovel, then the hammer claw without a handle, then rusty nails in an old torn paper sack, and two small empty boxes tools had once occupied. And then—there they were. His old shoes. Nike sneakers. Once, a long time ago, white—now red with dirt from our undeveloped, unlandscaped yard. Dotted with splashes of dark paint the color of the trim on our old house. Splotched with blue from painting the porches on our new house. Matted with sawdust and mud from building steps and handrails in December to please the county inspector. Filthy, ugly, worn-out shoes that I had asked him to throw away a dozen times, but which he kept and wore and cherished. I think he never threw anything away. He was one of those you-never-know-when-you-might-need-it persons. But now he was gone and he didn't need these shoes and I could throw them away right now. Into the garbage. Poof!

Then I looked at them and saw the years of work—the painting, the remodeling, the building, the repairing, the digging, the sawing, the installing, the creating. So much of what he was and how he lived, and all the things he could do and loved to do were in those old shoes. And now nobody was in those shoes. And no one, I thought, could ever be in those shoes. He walked in them strong and able and confident. How ironic that these ugly old shoes were still here and he who walked in them was gone.

But—the decision was mine. I could throw them away now—if I wanted to. I *should* throw them away. Nothing was stopping me.

I set them carefully on top of the garbage and shut the lid. I waited. But I could not do it. I lifted them out and held them and loved them and cried for the man who had walked in them.

As I hugged those worthless shoes, I tipped them slightly and a tiny stream of what I thought were pebbles flowed downward from the toe of one shoe. The shoes had little rocks in them, I thought, from past digging and gravel spreading. I looked more closely. No. Not rocks at all, but pine nuts deposited by one of the squirrels in our woods—quite a lot of nuts— enough to last a frugal squirrel several days, perhaps a week.

Well—did I think those shoes worthless? Ha! Dar and the squirrels knew better! The shoes' usefulness was never questioned by my husband. And now his view was borne out by nature.

I set the shoes back where I had found them. They were much more needed as a safe

∽∘∾

place to stash a squirrel's winter food than to adorn a smelly garbage dump. And somehow I am less sad, more reassured by this connection with nature. It pleases me, and I know it would please Dar, to know that a beautiful wild gray creature now walks in his beautiful old shoes.

What is lovely never dies

but passes into

other loveliness....

THOMAS BAILEY ALDRICH

The Comfort of a Cold, Wet Nose

Barbara Baumgardner

hadn't even wanted the dog in the first place! My husband insisted I get him to replace the dog that had died recently.

Soon, he was "my dog," a friend and faithful companion; not asking for any more than I was willing to give—a daily meal, a kind word, a warm bed.

But not my bed! No dogs allowed on my bed.

The night after my husband died, I lay there, staring into the darkness, my pillow soppy wet with the unending flow of tears.

∽o∽

The bed seemed so big all by myself and I was wondering how long it takes for a good case of loneliness to heal when I first felt it move. It was cold and clammy and creeping at a very slow pace into my open hand outside the covers. The solidified jellylike mass was followed by prickly hairs and just before I screamed, a muffled but familiar whine came from the creature that was forcing its cold, wet nose into my trembling hand.

"Oh, Shawn! What are you doing on my bed?" I threw my arms around his thick hairy neck and hugged and hugged.

In the days and months to follow, I came to realize that this dog I hadn't wanted was a gift of love from God. He was a warm fuzzy on my bed every night; a companion always willing, wagging, and available to go for a walk when I needed to get out of the house. Twice, he snapped at me as I wailed loudly and out of control, as if to reprimand me to be strong and of good courage.

Shawn taught me all about love and acceptance and forgiveness. That crazy dog loves me just as I am. And so I've learned to be a warm fuzzy to those around me who are hurting and

∽o∾

to approach them gently, loving them just as they are. Like my dog curled up by the warm fire, I just want to be there in case I'm needed. I thank God for providing a friend when I felt alone, and for the comfort of a cold, wet nose.

No burden is too heavy
when it is carried with love.

ANONYMOUS

Just as there comes

a warm *sunbeam* into every

cottage window,

so comes a *love-beam* of God's

care for every separate need.

NATHANIEL HAWTHORNE

Thanks for the Miracle, Sis

Jann Mitchell

from *The Oregonian*

*M*y Dear Sister Sally,

This is a thank-you letter, shared in public because—as you say—it may hold hope to others.

When I left you in the rehab center in mid-November, a week and a half after your second stroke, at age forty-six, you were paralyzed on your left side, confined to bed, confused about what was happening. Doctors said you could die, or at best subsist with extensive brain damage.

Thank you for proving them wrong.

Oh, the joy of having you and our younger sister, Jill, meet me at the airport in mid-January, just two months later! Precious, upright you—leaning on your cane, your hair freshly cut and styled, and tears running down your face. Were your cheeks wetter than mine?

We came to make sure that you would be safe at home alone until your son got home from school and your husband home from work. Those few days showed us you would and taught me far more than I can tell you.

Sure, you still have weakness in your left arm and a slight hearing loss. You mispronounce some words and get confused if we talk too fast, but you are intact: your keen intelligence, your delicious sense of humor, your thoughtfulness and generosity, your sweet soul. More folks should be as whole as you are.

And now we see a new side to the shy and sometimes fearful middle sister who preferred to stick close to home, while Jill and I ventured forth and got into trouble. Thank you for your example in courage, fortitude, and the ability to keep putting one foot in front of the other in the face of great odds.

I watched you exercising several times daily to strengthen your left arm: stacking dice and paper cups, moving a dish towel around the table in figure eights, laboriously picking up paper clips and small screws to drop into a cup.

I saw you punch numbers into the automatic teller machine to get your bank balance, then do it all again when you forgot the sum. And I was suddenly ashamed that some days simply getting out of bed seems like too much work.

Thank you for the laughter. When you go to have your blood checked weekly to make sure your blood thinner's working, you say you have an appointment at "the vampire's." When you looked at the bleak hospital photos I'd snapped of you attached to snakelike tubes, you said, "I was really having a bad hair day!" Boy, are you a lesson in lightening up.

Stopping by your office gave us the opportunity to see how much others care about you (something some folks never discover until a funeral). Your coworkers told me how helpful you'd been when their relatives suffered strokes. They talked about your enthusiasm and generosity when they had babies, or adopted a family at Christmas. Such an outpouring of love!

Several times you apologized for "being trouble." Don't you know how grateful we are, dear Sally, to finally be able to give back to you? Who else but you would present Christmas gifts in January—gifts you'd purchased long before the stroke, now wrapped in paper bags with bows because you couldn't manage gift-wrapping?

Thank you for pointing out what's truly important—and for saying that you've dropped from your list nagging your teenager about his room. "I used to worry about things I thought were problems—like being fat," you said. "Fat isn't a problem. Being healthy is the most important thing in the world." Let me remember that the next time I climb on the scale.

And thanks, too, for the lesson in gentleness with yourself. When you pulled your shirt on inside-out and we called it to your attention, you didn't beat yourself up for making a mistake as the rest of us do so often when we don't do something perfectly. You simply said, "Oops, I flunked shirt!" and fixed it.

I'm the wordsmith, but you say things better. Like when you read through all the nice letters that readers sent when I wrote about your stroke. "People are really nice, aren't they?" you said through tears. And over cocoa, you remarked, "I'm so glad I didn't die. I woulda' missed you guys."

We would have missed you, too, Sal. But I want you to know: As painful and as frustrating as this whole experience has been for you and everyone who cares about you, it has been rich in love and lessons. I'm thankful for that.

Because of you, I'll be more patient with the person walking slowly in front of me, or trying to figure out change. Who knows what odds they contend with, that stranger who is someone's father or mother or sister.

And I'm glad you're mine. My miracle sister.

I love you,
Janny

🌱

A Prayer

Not more of light, I ask, O God,

But eyes to see what is;

Not sweeter songs, but power to hear

The present melodies;

Not greater strength, but how to use

The power that I possess;

Not more of love, but skill to turn

A frown to a caress.

FLORENCE HOLBROOK

Gratitude

Be grateful for the kindly friends that walk
along your way;

Be grateful for the skies of blue that smile
from day to day;

Be grateful for the health you own, the work
you find to do,

For round about you there are men less fortunate
than you.

Acquire the grateful habit, learn to see how blessed you are,

How much there is to gladden life, how little life to mar!

And what if rain shall fall today and you with grief are sad;

Be grateful that you can recall the joys that you have had.

EDGAR GUEST

A Simple Gift
of Comfort

Jane Kirkpatrick

Women sat and stitched. Their worn and wrinkled fingers pulled together pieces of her past cut into little squares: a child's worn dress, a bedroom curtain, a flowered tablecloth (with the berry stain her husband made one holiday cut out and now discarded). Dozens of memories they patched together.

They sewed the single-colored backing down. The comforter, completed, would keep her warm through winter's winds.

What comforts are the memories, the patches that mark the past and then are held together with the stitching hands of friends placed over solid backing. Surrounded by the fondness, we recall the memories, let them nourish us, keep us warm, and give us much needed sleep; knowing in the morning we can set aside the quilt, rested, still wrapped in comfort.

In these difficult days, I give my comforter to you. May the memories you wish to savor wrap themselves around you, stitched together by the hands of friends.

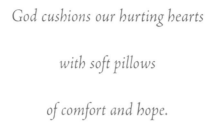

God cushions our hurting hearts

with soft pillows

of comfort and hope.

JUDY GORDON

Acknowledgments